EUROPA ⚔ MILITARIA N°9

82ND AIRBORNE DIVISION

IN COLOUR PHOTOGRAPHS

TEXT AND PHOTOS BY

MIKE VERIER

Windrow & Greene

LINEAGE & HONORS

Deep among the pines and dogwoods of North Carolina lies the vast military facility centred on Fort Bragg. Bragg is home to a unique formation within the US forces: the only divisional-strength organisation with an airborne 'forced entry' capability, its mission can be summarised with deceptive simplicity: 'Go anywhere - get in first - and win!'

The 82nd Division can trace its lineage back to World War One. Originally composed of draftees from Alabama, Georgia, and Tennessee, the 28,000-man division soon came to include soldiers from every state in the Union - hence the title 'All Americans,' and the red, white and blue 'double A' symbol.

Service in France produced a proud record, including the remarkable feat of Corporal (later Sergeant) Alvin C. York, who on 8 October 1918, with all his officers killed or wounded, took command of his platoon and single-handedly charged a machine gun nest. During the course of the action he killed some 20 German soldiers, and so demoralised the rest that four officers and 128 men surrendered their weapons and allowed him to march them into captivity. Corporal York was deservedly awarded the Medal of Honor.

Following war service the 82nd was reduced to reserve status until 1942 when its country needed it once again.

Under the leadership of the redoubtable Gen. Omar Bradley the erstwhile infantry division became the first of the Army's new airborne divisions. Having noted with alarm the effectiveness of Kurt Student's 'hunters from the sky' - the Fallschirmjäger - the Allies had moved quickly to imitate and improve on their tactics and equipment. Like the Germans, Allied paratroops were essentially light infantry, dependent on their unique 'three-dimensional' mobility to achieve their objective. This was not a new concept: in 1784 Benjamin Franklin had observed: *'Where is the prince who can so afford to cover his country with troops for its defence, as that ten thousand men descending from the clouds, might not, in many places, do an infinite deal of mischief before a force could be brought together to repel them?'* - thereby encapsulating in a single sentence the raison d'etre for parachute soldiers.

In the 1940s there existed neither the vast transport aircraft of today, nor the modern helicopter. Consequently only the spearhead soldiers dropped from the C-47s; others, more or less fortunate depending on your viewpoint, followed in gliders - an effective if somewhat hit-or-miss method of delivering large numbers of men to the battlefield. Once committed, the sky soldiers proved to be effective and tenacious warriors; North Africa, Normandy, the Ardennes, Holland and the Rhine all feature in their battle honors.

The end of the war in Europe saw the Division take up occupation duties in Berlin. As is so often the case with élite units, the 82nd set out to prove that when the fighting was over they could out-bull everyone else too. Thus it was that a welcoming review for Gen. George S. Patton prompted the remark: 'In all my years in the Army, and of all the honor guards I've seen, the 82nd honor guard is undoubtedly the best' - and gave rise to the Division's other sobriquet, 'America's Guard of Honor.'

The world was hardly less tense post-war than it had been prior to VJ day; and the 82nd, designated as part of America's strategic reserve, began the evolution into the form we know today. The fear of an opportunist Soviet offensive in Europe during the Korean War was largely to keep the paratroopers out of that conflict, their very combat readiness being good reason to hold them back. Instead the men of the 82nd spent much of the 1950s in intensive training from the arctic to the tropics so that they might be ready if the worst came. It very nearly did in 1962, when President John F. Kennedy confronted Chairman Kruschev over Cuba, elements of the Division being chuted-up for a possible combat drop at one point.

The 1960s were to see far-reaching changes, both politically and within the Army. Unrest in the Dominican Republic led to a successful deployment by the 82nd in 1965. Meanwhile, storm clouds gathered over South-East Asia.

The attention of military planners was moving away from parachutes; although jump-capability was always retained, the buzz word of the time was 'airmobile.' Airmobile, as opposed to Airborne forces, do not use parachutes; deployed strategically, they move about the battlefield by helicopter. Until then something of a novelty with little practical application beyond casualty evacuation, the helicopter was to come of age during the 1960s. The advent in 1958 of Bell's UH-1 (originally HU-1 and thus forever 'Huey') was at last to provide a helicopter of sufficient performance to lift a squad and transport it at high speed over a considerable distance. Vietnam was to be the 'helicopter war'; and, as ever, the troopers of the 82nd acquitted themselves well when called upon. Sadly, their best efforts could not prevent a political loss of faith at home, and the increasing unrest of the late 1960s led to troopers of the 82nd being committed to internal security duties in the urban United States. This is probably the most demanding task a regular soldier can face, and only those with the highest discipline and self-control are suitable. During this most difficult era the 82nd coped as best it could with such missions, and quietly got on with the business of training as part of America's quick-

reaction force.

In 1983 the constant training and preparation paid off. The mission requirement is to be 'wheels-up' in 18 hours; the 'All Americans' were on the way to Grenada in ten. The details of Operation 'Urgent Fury' are beyond the scope of this introduction, but as far as the 82nd were concerned it involved a speciality of theirs – 'airfield take-down'. Dropping from the big C-141 transports, the troopers of the Division quickly secured the airfield at Point Salines; and, with more men and equipment arriving by the hour, set about neutralising the opposing, and unexpectedly well-armed, forces. That this was accomplished so well is a matter of record. Attempts to portray the operation as an 'invasion' found little credence with the locals, who were only too pleased to see US forces. It proved equally difficult to perpetuate propaganda about 'racialist' Americans, given the number of black officers and NCOs in the Division – not to mention the sight of a crusty black sergeant vigorously questioning the parentage and intellectual abilities of an unfortunate white soldier who had 'screwed up'!

Grenada also proved the efficacy of two new pieces of kit for the 82nd: the UH-60 Blackhawk helicopter (which had replaced the ubiquitous Huey) and the Kevlar® helmet. The Blackhawk was found to be capable of absorbing considerable battle damage and still performing as advertised; while the 'plastic pot', at first regarded with some suspicion by the troopers (and christened the 'Fritz' on account of its decidedly Teutonic shape) did much the same on a more personal level. As a result the unit museum now displays one helmet complete with an embedded AK-47 round and a testimonial from its satisfied owner.

With the exploits of the British paras and commandos in the Falklands still fresh in the public consciousness, 'Urgent Fury' dispelled any further doubts about the need for forces capable of rapid intervention missions. In both cases a combination of Marines and Airborne had proved pivotal, a fact not lost on the 82nd. There followed a period of consolidation and training for the Division, punctuated by frequent deployments and jumps, including the somewhat prophetic 'Bright Star' exercises with the Egyptians (which gave the opportunity for further extending the already considerable range of foreign parachute wings worn by various individuals around Fayetteville...)

The Airborne were once again to hit the headlines in December 1989 when American tolerance of General Noriega's regime in Panama finally ran out. Operation 'Just Cause' was mounted to bring him to justice and restore democracy to the country. All arms of the US forces were of course involved, as the aim was to convince the dictator to surrender by an overwhelming demonstration of military might, coupled with superior technology. As ever the 82nd were in the thick of it, and dealt effectively with the resistance encountered. As in

(Above) Divisional commander Gen. Richard Timmins inspecting officers of the 2nd Bn., 504th Parachute Infantry Regiment. Students of insignia only get to see a soldier's full credentials when he wears service uniform – 'greens'. The lanyard of the Belgian Croix de Guerre was awarded in World War Two. Most junior leaders in Airborne and Light Infantry formations are required to qualify for the 'Ranger' tab, and the Division's spearhead role is indicated by the combat jump wings and Combat Infantryman Badge worn by several of these officers. Officers wear the regimental crest on the shoulder straps, and their rank on the beret, backed by a unit-colored patch – here that of the 504th, with two black bars indicating the battalion. A green loop on the shoulder strap indicates a Combat Leader.

The red beret, first worn by the British in 1942 and now the international symbol of paratroopers, was authorised for local wear in 1973 and donned for the first time on 31 August. The original maroon 'Denmark beret' was worn until 1979 when the US Army banned all unofficial headgear in the name of standardisation. This situation, clearly intolerable, lasted until November 1980 when the Airborne got their beret back; it was made their official headgear a year later, in a type known as 'Royal Artillery red'.

Grenada, the Division deployed a number of new equipment items, and for the first time in combat made extensive use of night-vision systems. The author can personally confirm the remarkable quality of American night vision goggles, which deny your opponent the cover of darkness; conversely, an enemy without such equipment is effectively blinded and quickly demoralised by night attack.

(Left) A Command Sergeant Major of 1st Squadron (Air), 17th Cavalry Regiment, part of the Division's Aviation Brigade; no less than eight three-year service stripes, Combat Infantryman, Master Parachutist and Pathfinder insignia, and ten ribbons headed by the Bronze Star all indicate a soldier to be reckoned with.

Technology also came to the fore with the first combat use of the AH-64 Apache attack helicopter. Designed to replace the AH-1 Cobra, the Apache is undoubtedly an awesomely capable machine, and it did everything asked of it during the operation. It is, however, a complex and very hi-tech item, and therefore prone to serviceability problems in combat conditions. While the manufacturers and the Army are now on top of most of them, this unfortunate tendency to vindicate Murphy's Law has led to some bad press, not all of which is justified. (The Apache's frightening effectiveness in the Gulf has silenced most critics.)

Attack helicopters also need scouts, and new OH-58Ds were deployed for this role. The Delta model '58, developed from the little OH-58A/C Kiowa, is almost a new aircraft; although it has a new engine and rotor system, it can most readily be distinguished by the mast-mounted 'ball' above the rotor disc. This contains the most advanced night vision system ever fielded, and enables real-time observation out to ranges in excess of 6,000 meters. At that distance, with just the ball above the tree line, the aircraft is invisible and silent. The enemy can run, but they can't hide...

Amid this welter of technology, Panama was also to see the first full scale combat commitment of a somewhat more mundane but vitally important piece of equipment: the Humm Vee, 'Grandson of Jeep.'

The invasion of Kuwait by Iraqi dictator Saddam Hussein on 2 August 1990 threatened nearly a quarter of the world's oil reserves, which lay under the sands of north-east Saudi Arabia only a few hours ahead of Saddam's tanks, defended by the kingdom's small and inexperienced army. On 8 August the first free world troops flew in to construct a hasty defensive line for the kingdom: the men of 3/504 Parachute Infantry. The days which followed saw the remainder of the 82nd pouring over the 'air bridge' spanning half the world; but before the arrival of the first Abrams tanks of the 24th Infantry Division (Mechanized) from Fort Stewart, Georgia, in the first week of September it was essentially only the lightly equipped paratroopers of the 82nd who stood in the enemy's path. By the time Gen. Schwarzkopf launched the ground phase of Operation 'Desert Storm' on 24 February 1991 the 'All Americans' had the company of many of the US Army's most powerful formations. They played a major part in XVIII Airborne Corps' fighting advance; and elements of the Division, operating alongside the French contingent, penetrated further west into Iraq than any other Allied troops, seizing the airfield of Salman on the extreme left of the XVIII Corps' hook into the Iraqi rear.

The 'All Americans'' performance in the Gulf has fully vindicated the Division's pride in its unique capabilities and role. Nobody can argue with the spirit summed up on T-shirts sold by the clothing stores lining Yadkin Road outside Fort Bragg: many feature a caricature 82nd trooper, armed to the teeth and festooned with ammunition and grenades, with the invitation: 'Intimidate THIS....'

THE DIVISION TODAY

The Division's proud history engenders a fierce sense of identity, immediately apparent if you visit Bragg. The paratrooper's red beret can be seen everywhere; and the streets bear names such as 'Bastogne' and 'Los Banos' (the latter commemorating a brilliantly executed raid to free POWs from the Japanese which went largely unreported at the time, being overshadowed by events on Iwo Jima). The largest local drop zone, DZ Sicily, recalls a rather more famous Airborne action, and is also the one into which the Division traditionally jumps on return from a combat deployment.

Like all élite formations the soldiers of the 82nd consider themselves special; they are, after all, the only Airborne unit still in role as paratroops, the rest being 'merely airmobile.' Consequently nobody says 'Yes, sir' – the correct usage is 'Airborne, sir!', to which the frequent response is their famous battle-cry 'All the way!'

As can be seen from the comparison tables, the Division has changed radically since the 1940s. While the mission remains essentially the same, the 82nd now wields more firepower than all seven wartime airborne divisions. Its reach is theoretically global and immediate, its autonomous capabilities immense. The Division has its own armor, artillery, and air-defense elements, all of which can be delivered by parachute alongside the troopers. Its helicopters can self-deploy if necessary, or be airlifted in once the airhead is secured.

The 82nd is also self-sufficient for personnel. Every member of the Division is jump-qualified, from the CG to the lowliest clerk, male or female. Fighting soldiers, even Airborne ones, still need cooks, supply specialists, medics, and even MPs. The US Army still excludes women from 'combat' specialities. They complete the same basic training as the men, however, including weapons proficiency, and are certainly expected to defend themselves if need be. (While the women are not expected to seek combat it cannot, of course, be prevented from coming to them, as was illustrated by the 'vigorous' response of some female MPs to hostile fire in Panama.) The women of the 82nd involved in 'Desert Storm' shared a common threat environment with the men. This author has no doubt as to their ability to cope.

(Top) 'Iron Mike' stands at an intersection at the very heart of Fort Bragg. Sculpted in 1961 by Leah Heibert, wife of the then Deputy Post Chaplain, the 15-foot bronze depicts the classic Airborne soldier of World War Two, and represents the spirit of the Airborne – proud of their history, but always looking forward, alert for any danger.

(Left) Airborne soldiers are, of course, a fit bunch; and every morning between 0600 and 0700, hundreds of men and women jog up and down Ardennes Road which runs through the Divisional area – in formation, complete with guidon-bearers and unit chants. The guidons are raised in salute when passing another group. There is considerable friendly rivalry between units for the smartest running strip.

Divisional Structure

The 82nd is part of XVIII Airborne Corps, which is also headquartered at Fort Bragg. XVIII Airborne Corps is the only organisation of its kind in the US defense establishment, and also exercises operational command and control over the 101st Airborne Division (Air Assault) at Fort Campbell, Ky.; the 24th Infantry Division (Mechanized) at Fort Stewart, Ga.; the 197th Infantry Brigade (Mechanized) (Seperate) at Fort Benning, also in Georgia; and the 194th Armored Brigade (Seperate) based at Fort Knox, Kentucky. Co-located at Bragg and also subordinate to the Corps are a number of other units which include Corps artillery, engineer, signal, support, military police, and intelligence brigades. Neither is it by chance that the JFK Special Warfare Center (together with the publicity-shy 'Delta Force') resides at Bragg, and much cross-fertilisation of ideas and techniques is evident.

The Division is built around nine infantry battalions, one of which is always at readiness for combat deployment and is known as the Division Ready Force. The DRF is one of four 'building blocks' of the 82nd's phased response system, which permits great flexibility in dealing with any mission. The smallest of these blocks would come from the DRF and is known as the IRC (Initial Ready Company): these are the scouts and artillery observers who go in ahead of the main assault. They keep their equipment ready at all times and can be chuted-up within the hour. The DRF would be expected to follow, and is required to be 'wheels-up' within 18 hours – though as noted already, much shorter times are achieved in practice. Aside from the infantry the DRF would also include an artillery battery, an engineer platoon, and possibly an MP squad. Helicopter crews are also assigned to it.

The penultimate 'building block' is the DRB (Division Ready Brigade). Comprising some 3,500 troops, it includes an anti-armor company, and an artillery battalion of 18 105mm guns. It would also be augmented with tanks, air defense, attack and/or cavalry helicopters depending on the nature of the mission. Finally, of course, the whole Division could be committed – with nearly 13,000 men the 'All Americans' potential for mischief is truly impressive.

In order to maintain this system each battalion cycles through one of three phases. The first and lowest state of readiness is known as 'post support.' Typically it involves low-intensity training and acting as aggressor units, or providing soldiers for the ceremonial duties so essential to military life. The second phase is one of intensive training, and is essentially preparation for the third, which is the DRF. The training culminates in a full strip-down inspection of every item of the battalion's equipment, following which it is declared ready for operations and assumes the 'number one' slot. Each of the nine battalions therefore moves progressively up the ladder. Should the DRF be assigned an operation the next battalion down will assume the role, and everyone moves up a notch in readiness. Soldiers in the DRF keep their kit packed, must never be far from a 'phone, and cannot go more than an hour away from the base without clearance. At least once during the duty period a no-notice EDRE (Emergency Deployment Readiness Exercise) will be run, which may go as far as a full-scale drop on a DZ almost anywhere in the world.

Today the Division is a truly élite force. Unlike the wartime and Vietnam years there are no longer draftees in the ranks; all the troopers have in fact volunteered twice – once for the Army, and once for the Airborne – both times undergoing rigorous selection. As a result the men of the 82nd rank alongside any of the world's finest units; and the British, French and other foreign jump wings on their chests are visible testimony to exchanges with many of them. Exchanges are a two-way street; amongst the first troopers deployed to the Gulf was a British Falklands veteran from 2 Para. (The very senior NCO in question caused world-wide amusement when asked innocently on live TV if he had any difficulty getting his American charges around to his British way of thinking. Back came the instant rejoinder: 'No trouble at all, ma'am – they come round, or I break their ***** backs.' Delivered with a perfectly straight face, this left the reporter with very little else to say.)

The proud heritage of the 82nd, its recent combat experience, and the quality of its training all ensure that today's Airborne troopers are highly professional and motivated; they know from their own history that freedom is a fragile commodity, and must at the last resort be defended by force of arms. There are few better equipped to defend it than the 82nd.

(Below) Of the specialties open to women the Military Police offers perhaps the most aggressive role. The 82nd has deployed women in areas of active operations since Grenada; this determined-looking trooper was photographed in Panama during Operation 'Just Cause'; and female members of the Division served with distinction during 'Desert Storm'. *(Photo: 82d AB)*

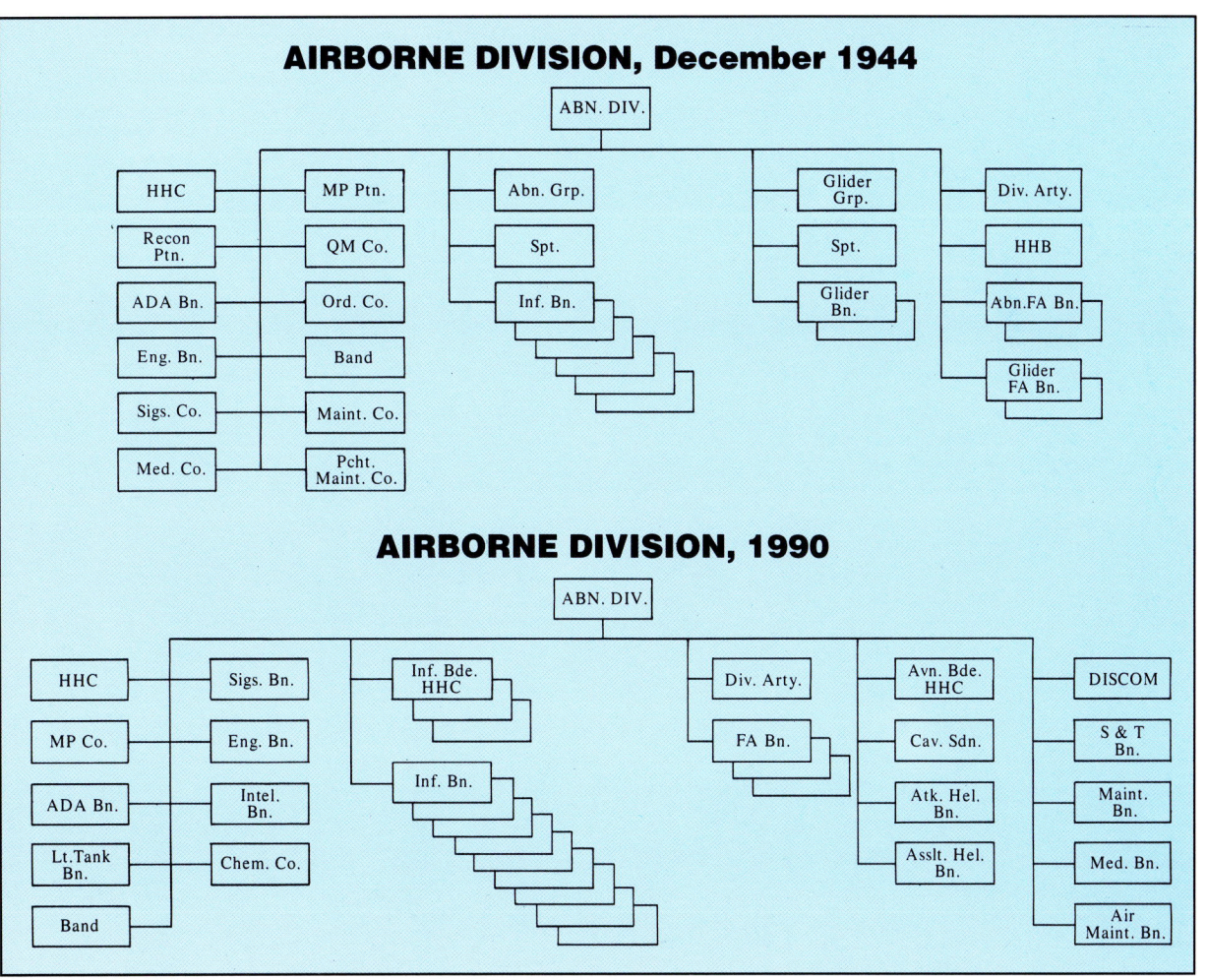

Sweltering in the fierce heat of the 'Green Ramp' at Pope AFB, troopers carry out final checks before embarking in even hotter Starlifters. The helmet tape is a DZ assembly aid.

AIRBORNE DIVISION, December 1944

- ABN. DIV.
  - HHC
  - Recon Ptn.
  - ADA Bn.
  - Eng. Bn.
  - Sigs. Co.
  - Med. Co.
  - MP Ptn.
  - QM Co.
  - Ord. Co.
  - Band
  - Maint. Co.
  - Pcht. Maint. Co.
  - Abn. Grp.
    - Spt.
    - Inf. Bn.
  - Glider Grp.
    - Spt.
    - Glider Bn.
  - Div. Arty.
    - HHB
    - Abn. FA Bn.
    - Glider FA Bn.

AIRBORNE DIVISION, 1990

- ABN. DIV.
  - HHC
  - MP Co.
  - ADA Bn.
  - Lt. Tank Bn.
  - Band
  - Sigs. Bn.
  - Eng. Bn.
  - Intel. Bn.
  - Chem. Co.
  - Inf. Bde. HHC
    - Inf. Bn.
  - Div. Arty.
    - FA Bn.
  - Avn. Bde. HHC
    - Cav. Sdn.
    - Atk. Hel. Bn.
    - Asslt. Hel. Bn.
  - DISCOM
    - S & T Bn.
    - Maint. Bn.
    - Med. Bn.
    - Air Maint. Bn.

GREEN RAMP

(Left) Fully rigged paratrooper on the ramp. Unusually, the Kevlar® helmet from the PASGT system is seen here uncovered; Airborne modifications are an extra internal pad and retention strap, and four sizes are available, from 2lb. 8oz. to 3lb. 4oz. weight. Below the manually-operated T10 reserve parachute clipped to the belly D-rings of the harness, the soldier's combat field pack is attached upside down; at about 200ft. altitude it is released and lowered on a 15ft. strap, so as not to hamper the landing – it also gives a useful last-moment warning when it hits the ground, especially during confusing night or water jumps.

(Below) Experienced trooper of the 35th Signal Bde. checks a trainee's rig.

A longside Fort Bragg is Pope AFB; the two bases are separate but totally interdependent for their mission. Pope houses squadrons of USAF C-130 Hercules tactical transports and C-141 Starlifters. When a jump is on the troopers assemble their gear and chute-up at Pope's 'Green Ramp.' There follows a sometimes long, hot wait until they can file out to the waiting aircraft. Parachutes and harness must be meticulously checked by the riggers to ensure that there are no malfunctions during the vital moments of the jump. Any item of loose gear flapping about would be a considerable hazard to men and machines, and all weapons and equipment have jump packs specifically designed to hold them secure.

Elsewhere the heavy gear, ammunition, and vehicles are palletised and transported to the aircraft. Normally this will be dropped moments before the troopers, so that the first men down can go directly to their vehicles and heavy equipment. There are a number of delivery systems for the heavier items which depend on the individual mission requirements as well as the terrain of the DZ. One of the more spectacular is LAPES (Low Altitude Parachute Extraction System), in which the aircraft skims the DZ and the load is literally yanked out by the deployment of parachutes. Items such as Sheridan tanks can be placed with great precision in this way.

(Top) The ALICE personal equipment is worn during the jump under the parachute harness.

(Right) Rear angle on 'No. 32', who obligingly posed in full jump rig for the author's camera. The standard T10B dorsal parachute pack, containing a 35-foot diameter parabolic canopy rigged to open 'canopy last', has its 15ft. yellow static line stowed in elastics. His rifle is carried in an M1950 adjustable weapons case; and note the jump knife strapped to the right inner leg. He wears standard BDU combat uniform with subdued divisional patch.

With modern positioning aids the force can be landed, at night, to within a few hundred yards of the target, thus greatly increasing its effectiveness and eliminating the fatal scattering often suffered by World War Two paratroops.

Once the airhead is secure the arrival of the Division's helicopters and other material begins in earnest. The mighty C-5 Galaxy can, for instance, accommodate a 'six-pack' of AH-64s. This, of course, is some time after the initial

(Above) After 'suppression' of the DZ is carried out by fighter-bombers, the heavy equipment and vehicles are dropped moments ahead of the first troopers. Here a C-130 demonstrates the Container Delivery System, which can put loads on a very precise objective day or night.

(Right & opposite page top) Items such as trucks are palletised; one is seen at the moment of impact, with another wave of C-130s boring in. The truck shown in close-up taught the author why the heavy stuff is dropped first: its arrival from directly above him prompted fast tactical withdrawal from an otherwise perfectly satisfactory camera position.

assault, and the helicopters have to be assembled after landing; but an exciting on-going development is the armed OH-58D. Bell have already demonstrated that with minor modifications for blade folding, etc., a fully armed '58 can be in the air less than five minutes after being pushed out of the aircraft. The demonstration was carried out at night, with a standard Army tool kit, and with only torches for illumination. With such a capable asset available almost immediately after the troopers hit and roll, the chances of success are considerably increased.

There are other methods of arrival practised by the troopers of the 82nd; most of them involve helicopters in one way or another, and include such delights as ingress by abseiling, and egress by the some-what undignified STABO rig developed to retrieve men from jungle too thick for the helos to land.

Hardly had the dust settled when the first sticks of troopers spilled from the Starlifters.

In a matter of moments all six aircraft in this assault had disgorged their loads – the last troopers came out the door before the first had hit the dirt, allowing the whole force to land with great precision in a comparatively small area.

(Above) Jumping in is only one of the several methods of arrival at which the 82nd are adept; during an airmobile exercise these troopers are exiting via the rear ramp of a CH-47 Chinook. Not for nothing is it called 'Big Windy': they wisely remain prone until it has lifted off, on the basis that if you don't, it'll blow you over anyway....

(Right) For the Rangers and recon types, there is always rappeling – the aircraft need to be rigged specially, and it is not suitable for large-scale assaults; but if the helos cannot get into a confined area, this is the best way in for small groups.

(Opposite) When said small groups wish to leave said confined area, the STABO rig – developed during the Vietnam War for extraction from otherwise impenetrable terrain – may be the only answer.

STABO extraction is said to provide a thrill all of its own....

(Opposite) A team leader photographed during 'Just Cause' in Panama, December 1989, armed with the M16/M203 rifle/grenade launcher combination and carrying its half-pound, 40mm rounds in a grenadier's vest; they have a range of 300 – 400 yards. Black rank insignia are worn on the collar of the BDUs, and subdued 'Ranger' tab and Division patch on the left shoulder, above a temporary flag patch for quick identification. This was particularly necessary in Panama, where many of the 'unfriendlies' wore US-supplied kit.
(Photo: 82 AB)

ARMS AND THE MAN

The 82nd's ultimate resource is the paratrooper, who has at his disposal a wide range of small arms as well as a variety of man-portable anti-armor and anti-aircraft weapons.

Much of his equipment is standard Army issue, and specialised 'Airborne' items are few, which simplifies logistics. (This practical but boring conformity perhaps accounts for the Airborne soldier's determination to wear his red beret at every opportunity...) Aside from the obvious parachuting equipment and jump packs for some weapons, the main visible difference between infantryman and paratrooper is the latter's helmet strap modification to make it more secure for the jump. The standard camouflaged 'BDU' (Battle Dress Uniform) is worn on most occasions, with matching helmet and PASGT body armor covers. Desert-camouflaged equivalents are issued as appropriate, in the 'kitty-litter' pattern now familiar to everyone in the world who owns a TV set. Personal equipment harness and packs remain in various shades of green, quite dark when issued but fading quickly in use.

The most widely used personal weapon is the universal M16A2 rifle with 20- or 30-round magazine. Whether or not a man carries a rifle he is issued an M9 bayonet; this multi-purpose item also functions as a combat knife, jump knife, and – with its special scabbard – as a wire-cutter capable of severing double-twist 11 gauge barbed wire.

Also designated M9 is the Beretta-designed 9mm semi-automatic pistol which has now replaced the much-loved .45 cal. Colt M1911 used by American soldiers for most of this century. The M9 is smaller, lighter, and of greater capacity than its predecessor (40.89oz. with 15-round magazine); but there is still some nostalgia for the Colt's legendary stopping power, claimed to be sufficient to bring a truck to a halt at close range.... The .45 cal. round has not entirely disappeared from the inventory, however, as the Division's Sheridan tanks still come with two M3A1 'greasegun' sub-machine guns for the crew.

Poor-quality photo, but a useful record of the M21 sniper rifle still in use in Panama. This accurised M14 in 7.62 caliber, with a 3-9x power adjustable ranging telescope, is in the process of replacement by the bolt-action Remington M24 with a 10x scope. *(Photo: 82 AB)*

(Left) The 5.56mm M60A2 machine gun, carried by both these troopers, is usually encountered these days in the platoon headquarters. The round black objects hung about the troopers' helmets and harness are the detectors for the MILES (Multiple Integrated Laser Engagement System), which uses lasers to accurately register 'hits' during exercises; the firing part of the system can be seen attached to the barrel of the right-hand M60. The detector triggers an audible tone when the wearer is 'hit', and the 'casualty' has to drop where he is. A marshal equipped with a 'God Gun' interrogator device will then tag the victim as dead or wounded, thus increasing the realism and training value of the exercise.

(Below) Moving off for what proved to be a three-day exercise, this trooper carries the 5.56mm M249 SAW (Squad Automatic Weapon) issued one to each four-man team in the rifle squad. This M249 is fitted with a box feeding a 200-round belt; the weapon also takes standard 20- and 30-round magazines for the M16A2 rifle, and so can be loaded at need by collecting clips from the squad riflemen.

Into the woods... This rear view shows a wide range of field equipment, and (right) the not inconsiderable extra burden of the MILES battery packs on helmets and body harness. Left foreground, the sustained-fire tripod mount for the M60 is carried on a trooper's large combat field pack, along with the plastic carrier for his entrenching tool; as an MG gunner he is issued with the M9 Beretta in its M12 holster. Several men carry the M72A2 LAW 'use and throw away' anti-armor weapon, issued as a round of ammunition.

(Above) Each rifle company headquarters has a mortar section with two 60mm M224 tubes. This man-packed 'pocket artillery' can throw up to 20 smoke, illumination or HE rounds in a minute.

(Left) Another rather poor posed photo from Panama shows the 81mm M252 mortar, of which four are issued to the battalion HHC; they are usually carried, with their five-man teams, on a Humm Vee, but can be broken down and man-packed if necessary. Range is 5,000 yards, giving useful fire support.

(Photo: 82 AB)

(Opposite top) 66mm incendiary rocket from the M202 FLASH four-barrel launcher striking a range target; the M202 has replaced the old flame-thrower in the Army inventory, and can also fire CS riot control rounds.

(Opposite middle, bottom left and right) Three frames separated by little over half a second, showing the moment of firing an M47 Dragon anti-armor missile. Its shaped-charge warhead is no longer capable of guaranteed penetration of the frontal quadrant of the latest generation MBTs, but it is still a serious threat to the majority of armored vehicles likely to be encountered.

(Above) Group of officers watching an artillery shoot. At left, an officer of the 82nd Aviation Brigade wears the standard Nomex® fire-resistant CWU-27/P flyer's coverall and MA-1 flyer's jacket; the helmet is mandatory during live firing, and the belt-rig and yoke are recommended in the field. The other three officers wear a mixture of standard BDU and (separately) the jacket and trousers of the issue rain suit.

(Left) Radio operator on the horn; he is using the AN/PRC-77 FM transceiver – in this case, part of the vehicle rig – and a pack-carried AN/PRC-74. Even for a comparatively simple exercise like this artillery shoot communications are vital for the smooth co-ordination of the artillery unit, its defensive infantry screen, the helicopters lifting the guns, and range control.

(Right) Two days after the troopers pictured on pages 23-25 assembled on a dirt road grid reference and set off into the trees, they finally got to make an assault on 'combat town' somewhere in the Carolina woodlands. By now half an hour has passed since the first wave hit the barbed wire simultaneously with the outbreak of a torrential downpour, and some men already carry the weapons of 'wounded' buddies.

(Below) SAW gunner anxiously scanning the next objective before his team makes its move out of cover during the painstaking house-to-house clearance of the town. Note, again, the MILES rig; and the slung anti-armor weapon.

(Left) These days it's not just a case of the umpire saying 'You're out!': casualties have to be handled like the real thing, and be CASEVACed off the battlefield, thus literally adding weight to the training. Despite the deluge and the fighting raging around them, stretcher teams must get the wounded out of harm's way.

(Below) The victim joins fellow 'casualties' in a Humm Vee ambulance. Normally they would be lifted from the nearest safe LZ by MEDEVAC UH-60s, but this morning not even the birds are flying; it's going to be a long ride back.

Half a world away from the red mud of North Carolina, the training pays off. This time the 'Ee-dree' is real – no 'ENDEX' signal, and no beer... This time the ordnance is live and the threat is genuine. Like every other time, the troopers of the 82nd proved equal to the task.
(Photo: Yves Debay)

(Left) The Iraqis laid hundreds of thousands of mines in the Saudi/Kuwaiti border zones, including the latest types from both Western and Eastern blocs, some virtually indetectable by electronic means. Mine training occupied many nerve-racking days during the months of 'Desert Shield'. *(Photo: 82 AB)*

(Below) The first formation to arrive in the Gulf, the Division trained relentlessly in a terrain more utterly empty than even the Mojave Desert military areas. During 'Desert Shield' more live-fire training was carried out than most peacetime soldiers get during their entire enlistment. Here the engineers' M67 recoilless rifle gets an airing out on the dunes; its 90mm HEAT rounds are used primarily for bunker-busting, and can penetrate 4ft. of concrete or 8ft. of earth. There is also an anti-personnel round. *(Photo: 82 AB)*

(Right) 'Mission Oriented Protective Posture 2' – a rain suit is worn by this 82nd trooper with the addition of gloves, M17A2 protective mask, and M6A2 hood. The mask has a 'voicemitter', and an integral tube which permits drinking when attached to the canteen's M1 NBC cap. Given the number of liters of bottled water the troops were ordered to drink daily in the Gulf, this was an essential item. When the Coalition forces surged over the Iraqi and Kuwaiti borders in the early hours of 24 February 1991 to initiate the ground phase of Operation 'Desert Storm' they all wore full NBC protection and carried masks and hoods at instant readiness; luckily, the chemical threat did not materialise. *(Photo: 82 AB)*

(Below) NBC training took on a new seriousness in the Gulf, as Saddam Hussein's chemical – and perhaps even biological – arsenal was a threat constantly held over the Coalition forces. Despite daytime temperatures of 120 degrees, all personnel had to practise carrying out their duties in chemical protection gear. Here, the worst nightmare of all is simulated: medical personnel train to give battle casualties immediate aid in a chemical environment. *(Photo: Yves Debay)*

(Above) Troopers of Alpha Company, 3/73rd Armor. The TC (left) has covered his issue DH-132 combat vehicle crewman's helmet with tape in camouflage pattern.

(Photo: Yves Debay)

(Left) A sand-camouflaged M551A1 Sheridan tank of the Division's recon unit, 3/73rd Armor, kicks up the dust of Arabia during one of the non-stop exercises to which the 'para-tankers' were committed from mid-August 1990 onwards: for nervous weeks they were the only US tanks in theatre facing enormous odds. By pure good luck the order to fly out caught them during training in California's Mojave Desert, so acclimatisation was easier than for many units.

(Photo: Yves Debay)

ARMOR, ARTILLERY AND ATTACK

Unlike its wartime 'infantry' composition, the 82nd Division today has its own organic armor and artillery for support. In addition there is the massive firepower of the attack helicopters available, all of which can be brought to bear quickly and accurately, day or night.

Unique to the division is the M551 Sheridan light tank. Actually designed to be air transportable, this 15-ton aluminium-armored AFV was conceived in the late 1950s as a result of the US Army's embracing of the 'airmobile' concept. First blooded – prematurely – during the Vietnam War, and subsequently seeing service in Europe, it did not have a particularly distinguished service career, and has been retired from all other regular units of the Army save for a few masquerading as Soviet vehicles at the National Training Center, Fort Irwin. Notwithstanding, it is still the only true *tank* that can be dropped from the back of an airplane – and that makes it ideal for the 82nd, who have 43 Sheridans in the Division's Tank Battalion (Light), currently the 3/73rd Armor.

The M551 has a number of interesting features, not least among which is the dual-role main gun which can either fire caseless 152mm ammunition, or act as launch tube for the MGM-57 Shillelagh missile. Shillelagh is now a 30-year-old system, but can still give the much more recent TOW a run for its money at maximum range of some 3,000 meters. The gun can fire a variety of rounds including HEAT-T-MP, WP, and canister, using combustible shell cases – a system much improved since its inauspicious introduction in Vietnam. Sheridan is also amphibious; and with no real replacement in sight (the Division has been trialling the LAV, but at present this lacks the firepower of the M551) looks certain to continue in the inventory for some time yet. For several tense weeks in August 1990 it was the only US tank facing down Saddam Hussein's legions of T-72s.

(Above) The M551A1 is admitted by the 82nd to be 'an old klunker' – the 3/4th and 1/11th Armor received it in Vietnam in early 1969 – but its combination of lightweight air-dropability, speed, amphibious performance, and very powerful 152mm gun make it perfect for the airborne armored recon role. Early problems with the electrics and the caseless ammunition have long been solved; only the massive recoil forces, which throw it about, remain a drawback from the maintenance viewpoint. The extra armored 'crow's nest' around the cupola first appeared in Vietnam, where crews liked to fit several external machine guns. Here a Sheridan of Bravo Co., 3/73rd lines up on the range.

(Opposite) 'Iron Eagle', 'Boss Eagle' and 'Screamin Eagle' wait their turn on the range. Fort Bragg has one of the most advanced tank gunnery ranges in the world, with moving, static, and pop-up snap targets, and electronic scoring facilities so that accuracy can be instantly assessed even at maximum range.

37

(Right) Sheridan's odd gun caliber is due to its doubling as a launch tube for the Shillelagh guided missile, also schemed for an M60 variant and the stillborn MBT70 project. Its main limitation is the time needed for the gunner to 'gather' the missile once fired, which makes it rather ineffective at short range. At maximum range of around 3,000 yards this 30-year-old missile can still compare respectably in destructive power with third-generation missiles like TOW.

The TOW missile system used by the battalion anti-armor companies is usually mounted on the Humm Vee. This impressive system is capable, in its improved versions, of defeating most current MBTs. It is also very effective against 'hard' targets such as bunkers, and being wire-guided is almost impossible to jam. TOW is also used by the Cobra attack helicopter, although the Army (unlike the USMC) made no provision for its retention on the next-generation aircraft, the Apache relying instead on the much more sophisticated and expensive Hellfire.

The Division's first line of defense against armor is, however, the attack helicopter fleet of 1st Battalion, 82nd Aviation Brigade. First developed during the Vietnam era as an essentially anti-personnel weapon, the attack helicopter has evolved into a deadly efficient component of the 'air-land battle.' Towards the end of the war in Vietnam the first TOW rounds were fired in anger from converted Hueys, the Cobra at that stage not being able to carry the sighting system; these were an immediate success (at Kontum, in May 1972) and a vast improvement over the unguided rockets previously employed.

'On the way!' – a Shillelagh seems to amble down-range by comparison with the sound and fury of firing a conventional round from the 152. Its arrival at the far end is rather more startling.

The classic Browning M2HB .50 cal. heavy machine gun, dating from the 1930s, is still a potent weapon against light armor, aircraft, and personnel. Although production ceased just after World War Two, stocks finally proved insufficient to keep up with world-wide demand in the 1980s, and the line was re-opened.

The Light Armored Vehicle (LAV), derived from the Swiss Mowag Piranha in 1985 for the US Marines, is on operational trial with the Airborne, and was used in the Gulf for recon work. Apart from its high speed (65-75mph on roads), amphibious capability, and air-transportability due to its 10-ton weight, it has space (albeit cramped) for up to six troopers; the riflemen can deploy under cover of the 25mm turret 'chain-gun', which fires both HE and APDS rounds. The main question is, of course, 'Can we push it out of an airplane that has not necessarily landed?' It is understood that some modification will be needed to achieve this. There are also variants for commanders, mortars and TOW launchers.
(Photo: Yves Debay)

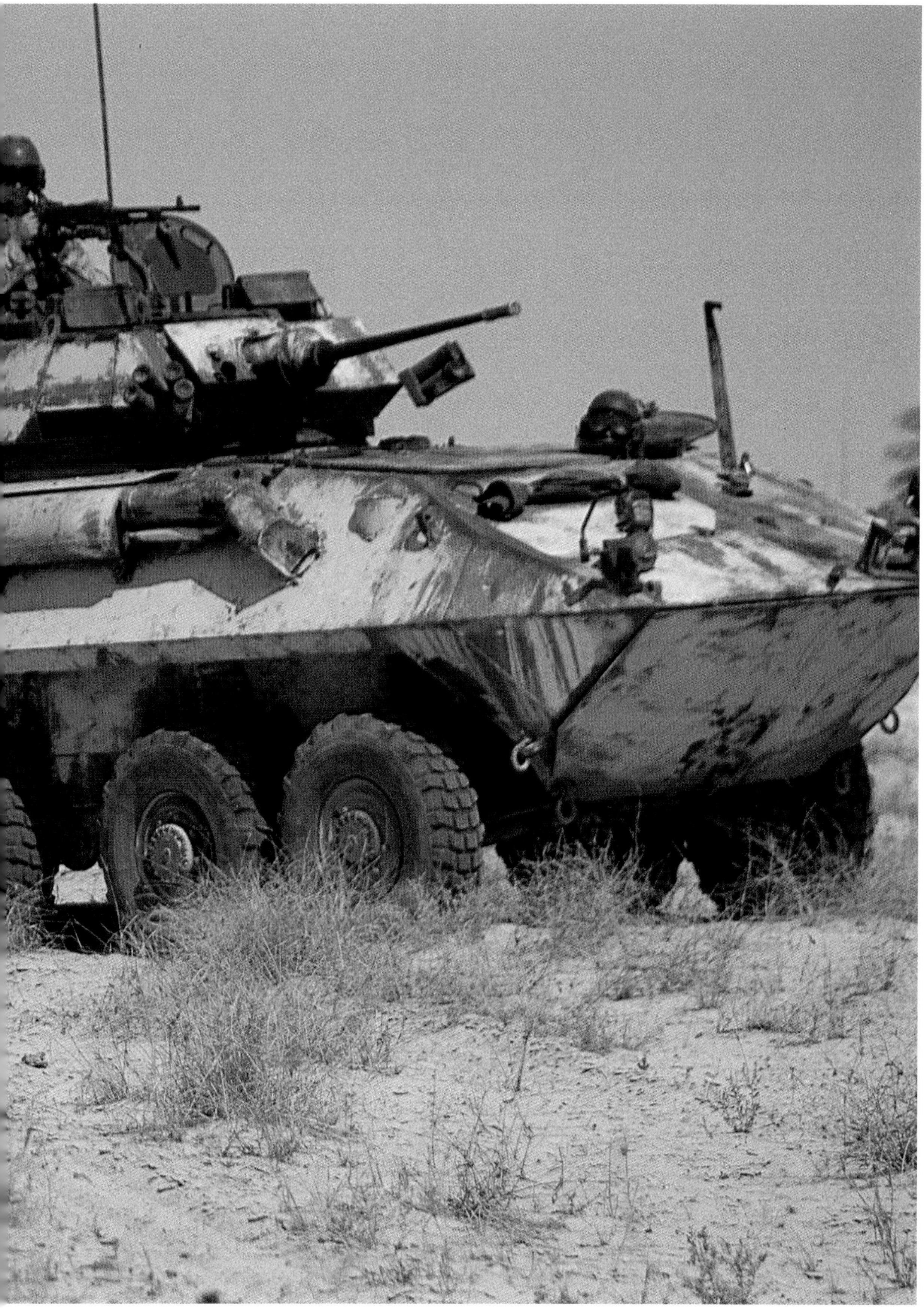

(Above) Divisional artillery officers deliberate before a shoot. The widely-seen helmet bands with two luminescent 'cat's-eyes' on the back allow troops to follow the man in front even on nights too dark to see their hands in front of their faces.

(Below) The TOW – wire-guided, and thus virtually impossible to jam – can be tripod-mounted as an 'infantry' weapon, though it is normally deployed on the ubiquitous Humm Vee. Dependent on visual guidance, it has a useful night capability via the AN/TAS-4 thermal imaging sight (seen here with the orange cover).

At least two attempts to design replacement aircraft for the 'interim' Cobra came to nought, and it was not until recently that the definitive production AH-64 Apache was fielded, first seeing combat in Panama as noted above.

An enemy armored formation would therefore first encounter artillery fire and attack from the air. They would also suffer 'sniping' from the highly mobile Humm Vee/TOW combination. Any survivors would then have to run the gauntlet of the Dragon teams, and finally the individual troopers with the AT-4 and LAW rockets. Few would penetrate all three layers of defense.

Mention of the Division Artillery brings us to some of the oldest units in the 82nd. The 319th Field Artillery can trace its connection with the 82nd Division all the way back to its original formation in 1917, and its three battalions make up the 'Divarty.' Each battalion has three batteries of six M102 105mm towed howitzers. Deliverable by parachute and transportable by UH-60, its prime mover is the Humm Vee (itself deployable by the same methods). Capable of firing a wide range of munitions out to 15,000 meters with rocket-assisted rounds, it can fire and re-locate quickly to avoid retaliatory fire; the artilleryman's prime directive is 'shoot, move, communicate.' The M102 is in the process of being replaced by the more modern and longer-ranged M119, a British design with a reach of between 14,300 and 19,500 meters. Anti-aircraft firepower is provided by the ADA battalion, currently the 3/4th ADA. Even older than the 319th, the 4th Air Defense Artillery's lineage includes battle honors from the War of 1812 and the Little Big Horn. The 3/4th ADA is equipped with the awe-inspiring Vulcan six-barrelled 20mm cannon and the shoulder-launched Stinger heat-seeking missile, in three mixed batteries each with nine M167 Vulcans and 20 Stingers. The Vulcan is a 'Gatling-type'

A clearing, almost anywhere...two UH-60s sweep in with a pair of 105mm howitzers and their crews. Things will move very quickly in the next few minutes.

rotary weapon first developed as internal armament for fast jet fighters; it has also been used vehicle-mounted, and as the basis of the shipboard Phalanx anti-missile system, and in its three-barrel form it serves in the Cobra attack helicopter. With a 3,000 rpm rate of fire it devastates anything it hits, and is therefore a useful direct fire ground weapon as well, efficient out to 2,200 meters.

The Stinger is an advanced man-portable anti-aircraft weapon which has proven its effectiveness in combat. It is also now mounted on a version of the OH-58 helicopter flown by the Division: originally intended to provide the little scout helicopter with a measure of self-defense against hostile aircraft, Stinger was found to be capable of use against surface targets too, and has proved to have offensive as well as defensive capabilities. Unconfirmed reports speak of 'effective' use against Iranian fast attack boats in the earlier Gulf crisis which led to US Navy escort of third-country tankers.

(Right) The guns are on the ground, unshackled, and troopers race to bring them into action as the Blackhawk lifts away.

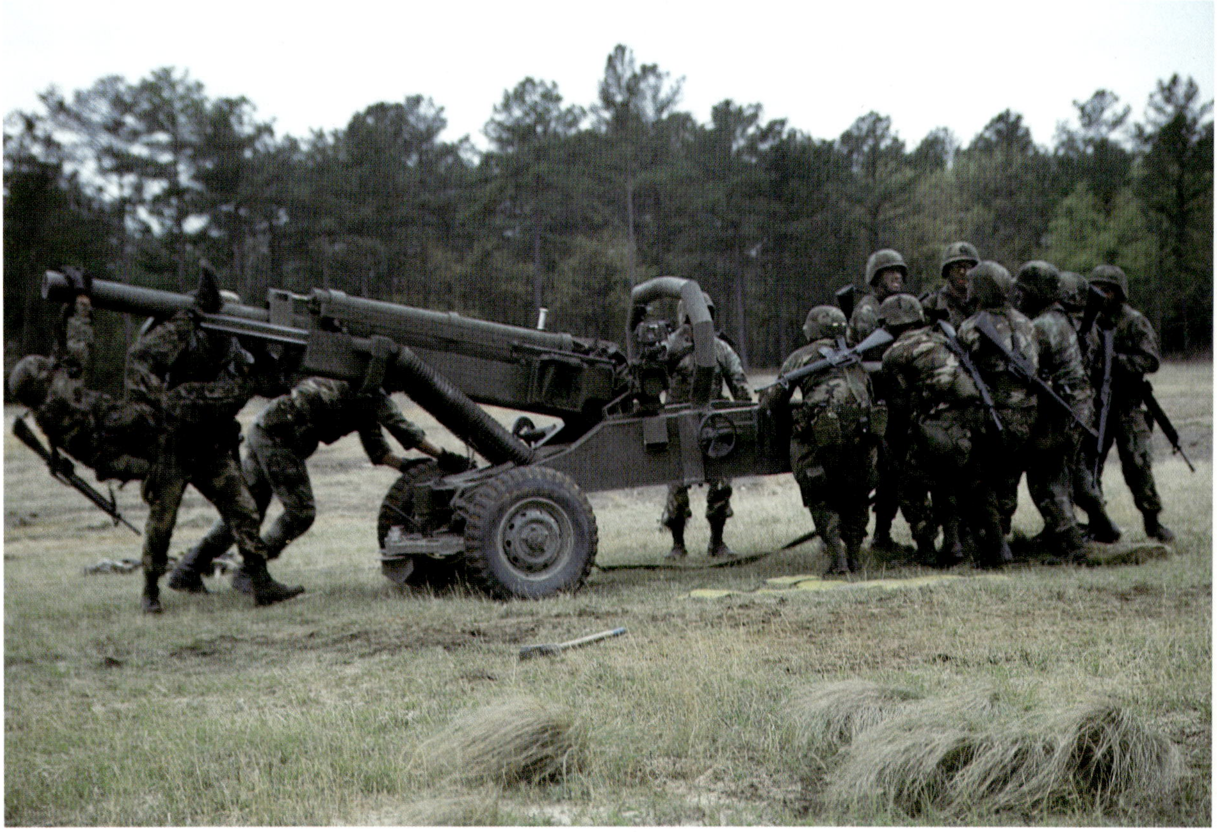

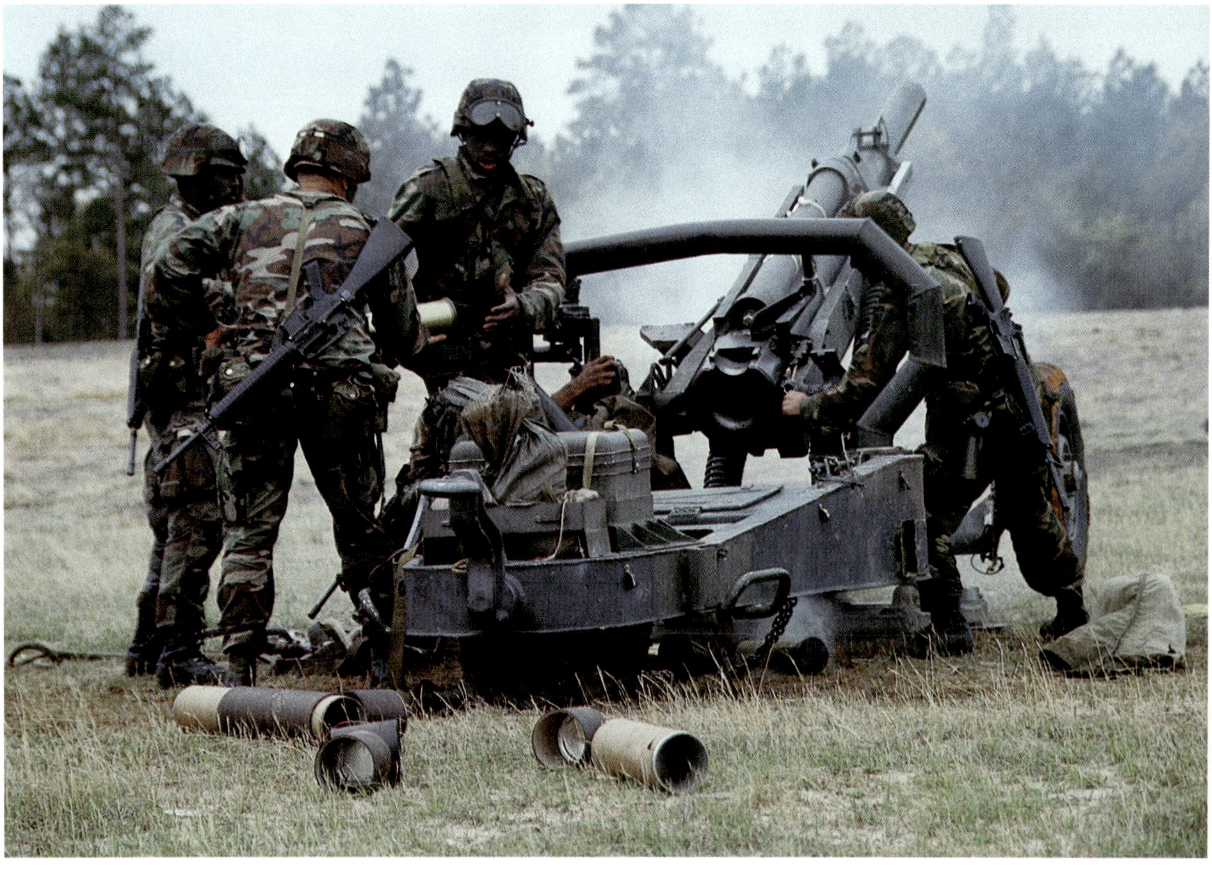

(Opposite top) The M102 is a lightweight, highly mobile weapon; while 'lightweight' isn't the word these men have on their lips at this moment, it nevertheless takes only a matter of seconds for the crew to manhandle it into firing position.

(Left) In rapid succession two rounds are fired, the second before the first has landed. With conventional rounds the M102 has a range of 11,000m plus; rocket-assisted rounds have a reach of 15,000 meters.

(Above) Before the enemy can locate the 'artillery raiders' the guns are stowed up for shackling and lifting again, and the helos swoop in to pick up the crews. In not much longer than it takes to tell the Airborne gunners have landed, fired four rounds at an unseen target, and moved out, leaving only echoes and drifting smoke and dust behind them. The essential mission of the old horse artillerymen is thus revived – with a hundred times the mobility and firepower.

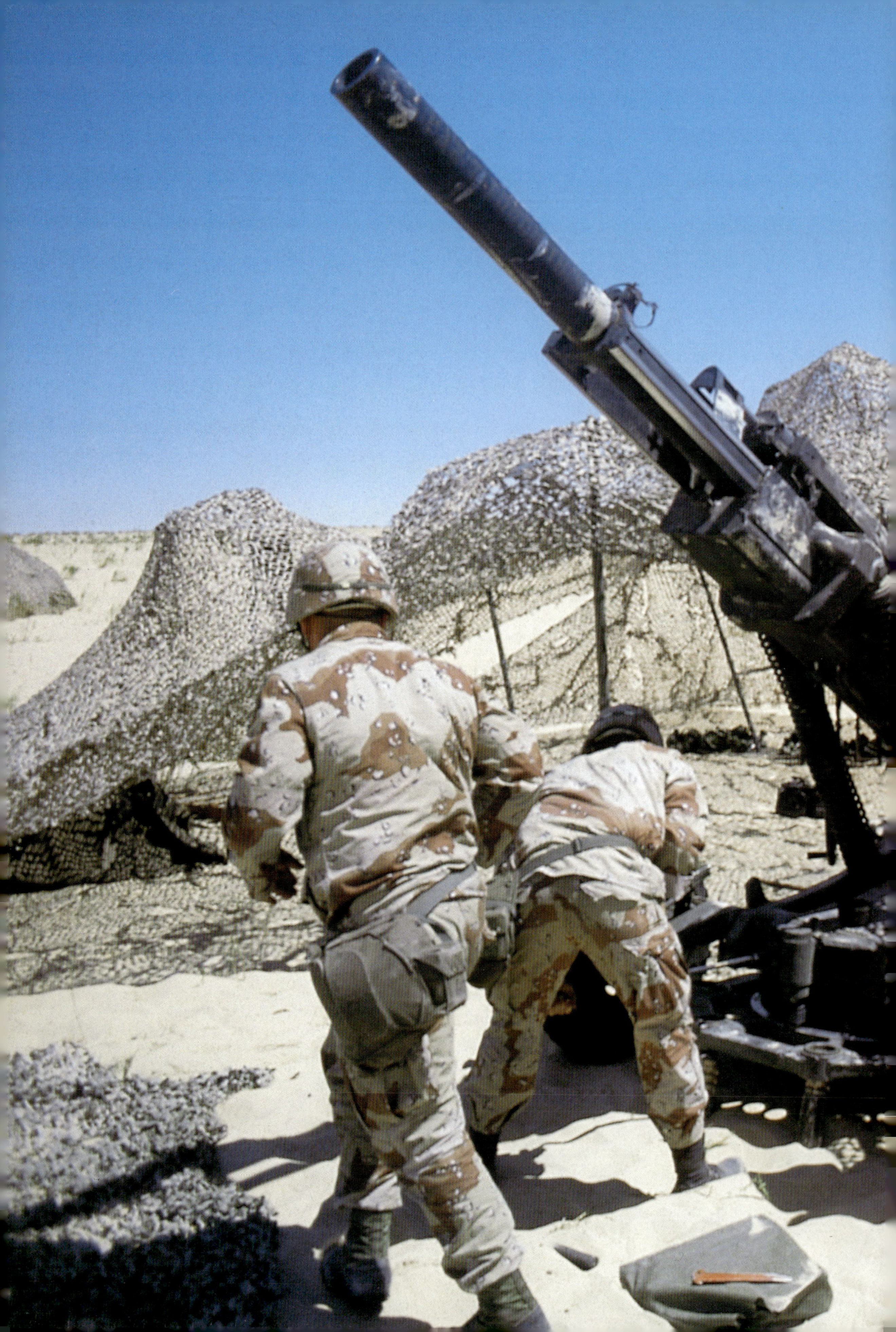

The real thing: somewhere near the northern border of Saudi Arabia, troopers of the 319th Field Artillery serve an emplaced M102 during Operation 'Desert Shield'. *(Photo: Yves Debay)*

(Above) The Vulcan gunner wears a standard aviation helmet rather than the tankers' CVC type.

(Left) The MLRS is not an 82nd Airborne divisional asset, but was deployed by XVIII Airborne Corps in support of the Division during 'Desert Storm'; this launcher vehicle is from B/3/27th FA. The 12-round M270 Multiple-Launch Rocket System, mounted on a vehicle derived from the Bradley and with a crew of three, has the firepower of whole batteries of World War Two artillery. Its 13-foot rockets, unguided but very accurate, have a range of some 18 miles; the M77 warhead scatters 644 anti-personnel, area-denial and HE sub-munitions over a wide area with devastating effect. The MLRS was highly destructive of Iraq's strong artillery assets during 'Desert Storm'.

(Top) The six-barrel M167 Vulcan 20mm cannon in its towed configuration. By now the US Army had planned to replace Vulcan with the 40mm DIVADS system (briefly and inappropriately named after the redoubtable Sgt. York); but its technical failure gave the M167 an extra lease of life. It is truly awesome in use, and the deep ripping sound of a 'Gatling' burst is quite distinctive; it is also highly versatile and mobile. In keeping with the 4th Artillery's status as one of the Army's senior regiments, the author was not allowed to photograph these gunners of the 3/4th ADA until the whole working party were properly dressed, with correctly-angled berets. The Brigade of Guards could have done no better.

(Above) The AH-64 Apache was once described as 'looking like it was waiting for its trainer to throw it some raw meat'. It certainly impressed the Iraqis during 'Desert Storm': on one occasion a pair of Apaches supported by OH-58s so mauled a bunker complex that nearly 500 enemy soldiers came out and surrendered. The somewhat surprised aviators continued to circle in predatory fashion until Chinooks arrived with back-up troops to collect the Apaches' cowed prisoners.

Primary armament is the Hellfire missile, of which up to 16 can be carried; in practice an operational mix would include the unguided 2.75in. FFAR seen here on the outer pylons. All four weapon stations are also 'plumbed' for fuel tanks; assymetric loading is possible, and one tank is sometimes carried to increase range without seriously degrading the warload.

(Right) Much attention has been paid to 'survivability'; Apache's engines are widely separated, and have exhaust plume suppressors to reduce the risk from IR homing missiles; there is also a jammer mounted aft of the rotor pylon. AN/ALQ-144 'disco-lights' throw out random heat signatures, to drive incoming seeker heads into a frenzy of self-doubt, and ultimately into giving up and going ballistic...

(Right) Apaches perform a 'pop-up' and fire pairs of 2.75in. rockets. Note the long-stroke undercarriage, armored cockpit, and secondary armament – a 30mm Hughes 'chain-gun' mounted below the nose as a suppressive weapon.

Progenitor of the AH-64 is the classic AH-1 Cobra. Armed with TOW rather than Hellfire, the Cobra can still provide a considerable back-up to the newer attack helicopter. Here the gunner is head-down at the TSU as he blazes away with the three-barrel M197 version of the 20mm Vulcan.

(Left) Despite the flat-plate canopy the late-model 'Snake' retains an elegance of line not found on subsequent attack types. This is in fact the penultimate model, once AH-1S and now redesignated AH-1E, which lacks the bulky exhaust suppressor of the fully modified aircraft. These airframes are colloquially known by the acronym for their modification state, ECAS (Enhanced Cobra Armament System). 'Ee-kass' refers mainly to the fitting of the 20mm gun, and an advanced composite main rotor blade distinguishable by its tapered tips. Some of the original 25-year-old airframes of this remarkable machine are still in service.

(Above) Eyes of the Apache: the little OH-58 I Kiowa, whose mast-mounted ball contains some of the most sophisticated 'visionics' ever fielded. So successful were initial trials at Fort Irwin that the boundaries of the exercise area had to be extended to prevent cries of 'foul' from opposing forces who had been observed all the way from their assembly areas and 'zapped' the moment they crossed the start line. The mast allows the helo to lurk below the treetops while it scouts the enemy.

(Left) It was not long before offensive capability was added to the OH-58's 'long eyes'. The OH-58D Warrior was developed, and deployed to the Gulf, in just 90 days during 1989. The then-secret Operation 'Prime Chance' against Iranian gunboats attacking civilian shipping was so successful that the threat was eliminated almost overnight. The '58 Delta' is so full of black boxes that it is now only a two-seater, and pilots speak of 'putting it on' rather than 'getting into it'. This example is fitted with Hellfire anti-armor missiles and a 2.75in. rocket launcher; many other combinations, including Stingers and gun-packs, are possible.

(Left) The Rockwell AGM-114A Hellfire had a protracted development, but finally proved its combat worth during 'Desert Storm'. It is a true 'fire and forget' weapon, laser-guided from a designator either on the launch aircraft or remote (on another aircraft, or operated by a team on the ground). Multiple targets can be engaged without the helicopter having to remain unmasked and vulnerable during the missile's flight time. The (classified) range of Hellfire is believed to be about 5,000m-plus; its primary limitation is thus the sensor capability of the launch aircraft. The combination of the OH-58D's advanced visual systems and a long-range, very accurate and highly destructive missile makes the inside of a tank several miles away a thoroughly unsafe place to be.

(Below) The 'ordinary' OH-58 Kiowa has acquired a pair of Stingers for self-defense. Apart from spare loads carried in the back, re-loads can be gathered from units on the ground, as Stinger comes pre-packed. Here CW3 Karl Ebert brings the Division's first OH-58CS low across Mott Lake.

(Overleaf)
(Inset left) The OH-58CS has a head-up display essentially the same as that on F-16 fighters. Here we are about to put the acquisition box on one of three Hueys which have unwisely skylined themselves. The word 'arm' denotes one missile left; in a moment an audible tone will indicate that the Stinger's seeker has acquired the Huey's heat signature. (The author's score currently stands at two Hueys and a Chinook...)

(Inset right) Karl Ebert hovers the Stinger-armed Kiowa close to the lake shore. Note the distinct lean to port due to the weight of the missiles.

(Main picture) Dawn: a Kiowa of the 82nd Aviation Bde. cruises a few feet above the treetops, hunting for trade.

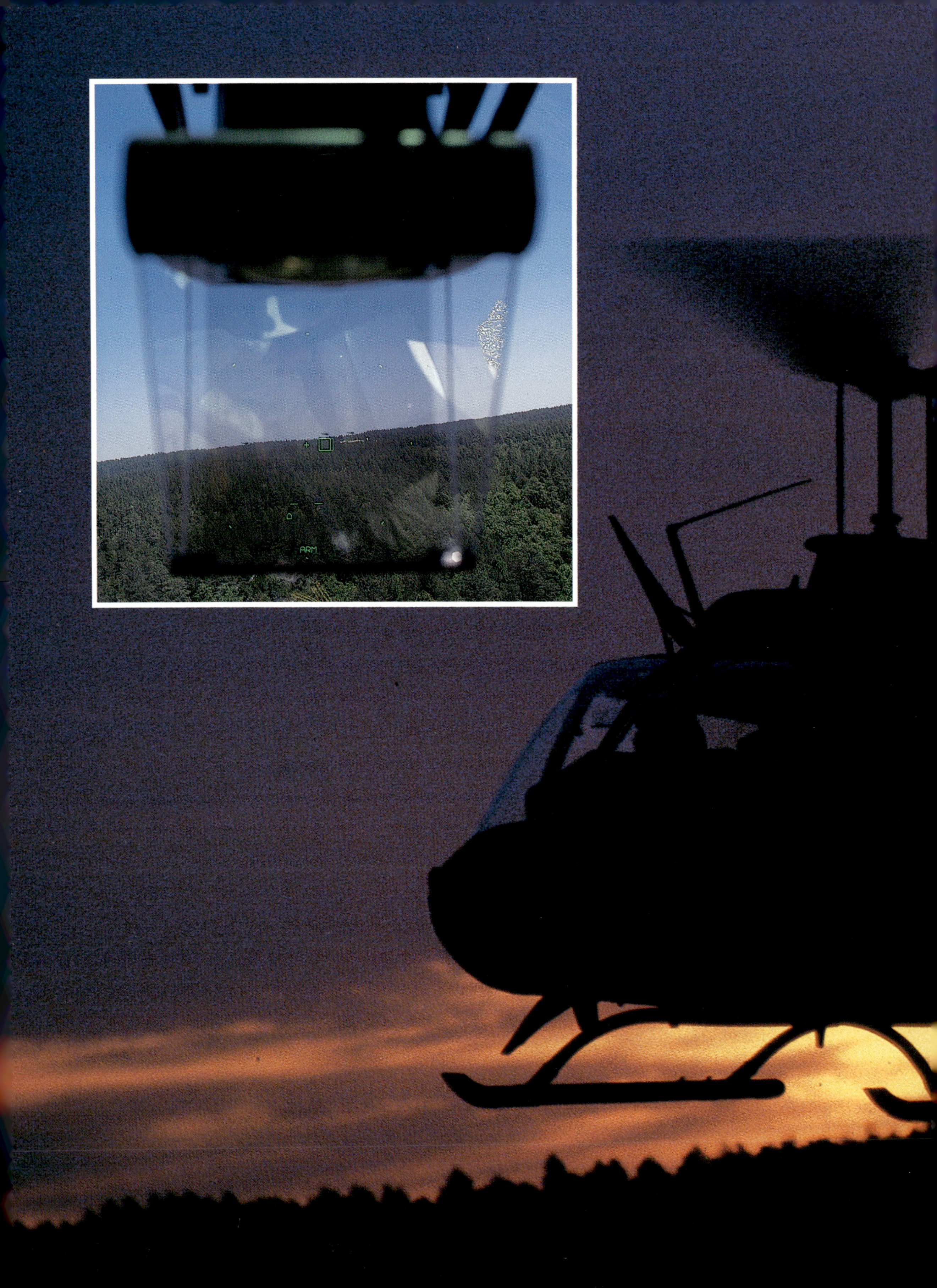
ARM

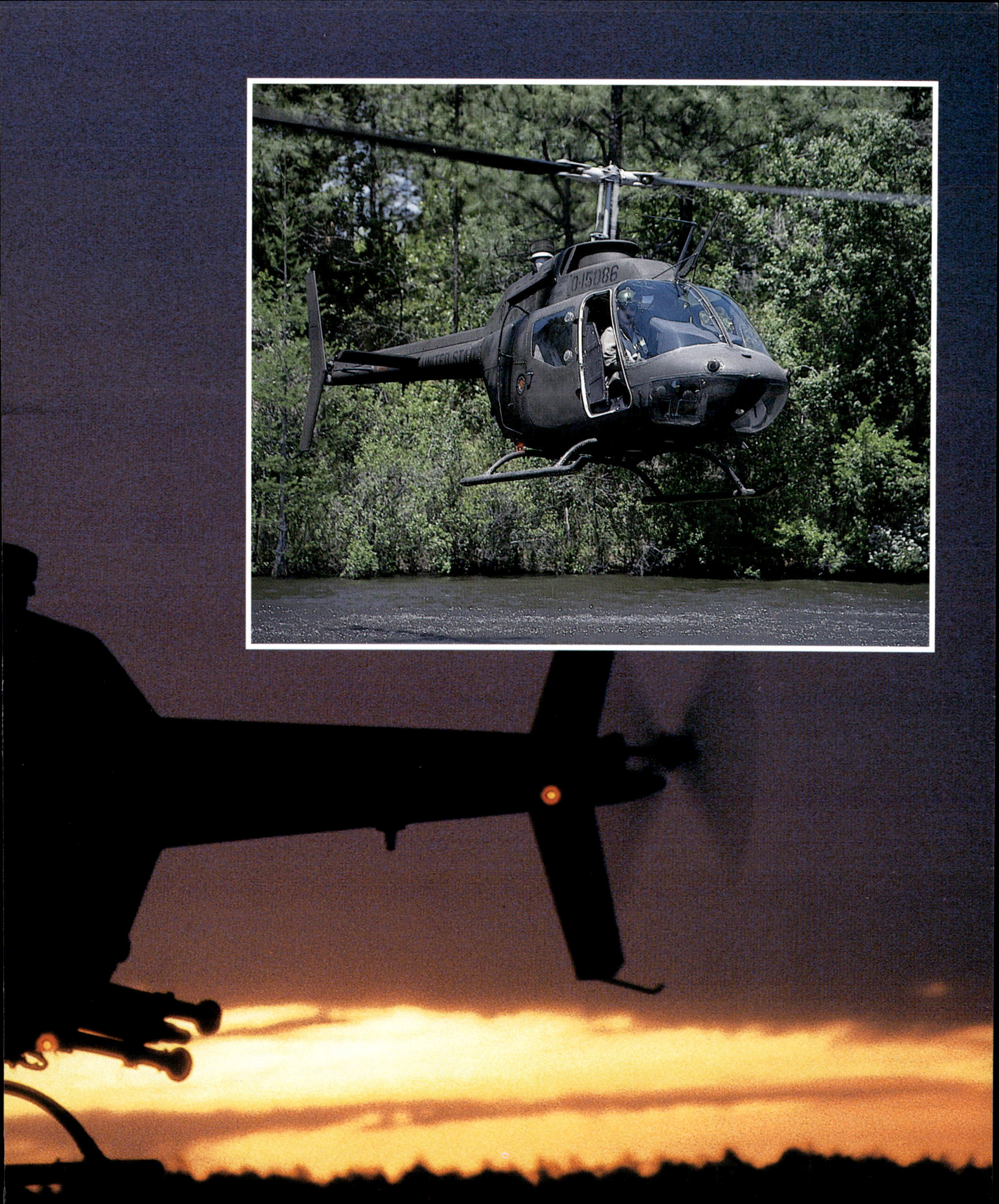

56

LIFTERS & SHIFTERS

(Above) Some idea of the sheer size of the C-5 Galaxy can be gauged as the behemoth points its 36 wheels at the Pope tarmac. It can carry a staggering 291,000lb. payload; and has the volume to accomodate virtually anything in the Army inventory, including the M1 Abrams MBT, and 'six-packs' of AH-64s.
It has recently been cleared for dropping paratroops; as the main hold could theoretically accomodate nearly 300 (there is an upper deck which can take 145 fully-equipped troops, but egress would not be quick enough for para-dropping), it would be a formidable addition to airlift capacity under the right circumstances.

(Left) At a comparative angle, the Galaxy's smaller brother – the C-141 Starlifter, the Division's primary transport for combat jumps of any size. Able to deploy world-wide with the aid of in-flight refuelling (as can the C-5), the aircraft can carry 168 paratroopers at jet speeds. Lockheed has 'stretched' most of the aircraft built to this C-141B standard; it was found that A-models ran out of volume well before they ran out of lifting ability.

The key to the effectiveness of the 82nd is mobility. The Division has near-global strategic mobility courtesy of the USAF, whose C-141 Starlifter and C-5 Galaxy aircraft can carry everything in the Division's inventory. The mighty Galaxy is the largest aircraft in the Western world, and statistics about it beggar the imagination. The one this author most enjoys aptly demonstrates the progress aviation has made in a single long lifetime: the fact that the whole of the Wright brothers' first flight could take place inside the C-5....

Tactical transport is provided by the USAF's ubiquitous C-130 Hercules, and by the 82nd Aviation Brigade's helicopter companies. (Both the Hercules and the Starlifter are due to be replaced by the yet-to-fly C-17 in the near future.)

Two helicopters dominate the 82nd's fleet: the previously mentioned UH-60 Blackhawk, and the heavy-lift CH-47 Chinook. Although now quite an old aircraft the CH-47 can lift prodigious loads both internally and slung externally. In service around the world its capabilities have become legend: a Chinook once lifted 147 Vietnamese refugees and their belongings. More recently (and rather more relevantly) 81 fully equipped British paratroopers were accommodated during the Falklands campaign – they were reported to have just kept marching in until no more would fit. The punchline of both anecdotes is that the advertised load is 44 fully-equipped soldiers....

(Above) The trio of Lockheed transports is completed by the faithful C-130 Hercules, the world's leading tactical transport type for over 30 years. It can carry most of the Division's equipment (including the Sheridan tank) into short, unprepared strips. These Hercs are not equipped for in-flight refuelling, unlike those in British service, thus emphasising their tactical rather than strategic role.

There are still some Hueys about; but the other most numerous type is the little OH-58, which serves in various forms for scout and liaison work.

Turning to wheels rather than wings, the vehicle that dominates all others at Fort Bragg is the 'Humm Vee', more properly the HMMWV (High Mobility Multi-purpose Wheeled Vehicle). Intended to replace the M151 'Mutt' – itself descended from the vehicle most associated with US forces, the Jeep – the Humm Vee is seen in an ever-increasing number of variants ranging through straightforward trucks to specialised radio, weapons, and ambulance versions. Its cross-country mobility is described as 'superb', and this author can certainly vouch for its ability to cross obstacles with apparent ease. Transportable as a sling-load by the UH-60, it is a truly tactical vehicle which goes where the troops go.

There are a variety of older trucks, wreckers and the like still in service, but those that aren't supplanted by the Humm Vee will eventually be replaced by another modern cross-country capable type known colloquially as 'Hemmet', the acronym in this case (HEMTT) standing for Heavy Expanded Mobility Tactical Truck. At present there are at least four variants in service including fuel, ammunition, and cargo. These enable essential supplies to be delivered to the front line in reasonable bulk instead of having to be broken down into smaller loads. The prime mover has become familiar to TV viewers as that used for the Patriot missile system.

Finally there is a range of 'C squared' (command and control) vehicles. Readily identifiable are the slab-sided M557 command post vehicles – the last M113 chassis vehicles in the Division; not so easy to spot are the host of communication, surveillance, and jamming systems that any modern army needs.

One that may be slightly easier to pick out is the EH-60 Blackhawk helicopter variant with its plethora of external aerials. Heart of the system is the AN/ALQ-151 countermeasures set, known as 'Quick Fix'. Essentially an airborne radio interception and jamming system, it has to be exercised with care – inadvertent selection of the wrong frequency can blot out every TV in Fayetteville.

(Right) The aircraft that put the 'air' into 'mobile': Bell's UH-1 'Huey' is still to be found in considerable numbers among the US forces, and the 82nd is no exception. This UH-1H just lifting out of OP5 shows the classic two-blade rotor and wide fuselage; it is little changed from the Vietnam years, when it literally revolutionised infantry warfare.

(Below) If ever there was proof of the fixed-wing community's belief that helicopters don't so much fly as beat the air into submission, the CH-47 Chinook is it. 'Wokka' or 'Big Windy' provides the Division's heavy lift capability; September 1991 sees its 30th birthday, and in the up-graded and more powerful CH-47D form shown here, about to pick up a truck as a slung external load, it is set to serve for many years yet.

A worthy successor to the Huey is Sikorsky's UH-60 Blackhawk, now almost universal within the Aviation Brigade in utility, MEDEVAC, and electronic warfare variants. The basic '60 can accomodate 11 fully equipped soldiers and a crew of three; in the combat assault role it mounts an M60 in the sliding windows just behind the cockpit on each side, leaving the cabin doors clear for the troopers on 'hot LZs.' A center line external cargo hook allows underslung loads to be carried without modification, and power from the two T-700 engines is enough to lift items such as the Humm Vee illustrated here. It also has provision for bolt-on stub wings (External Stores Support System) with four racks, usually carrying four external fuel tanks which vastly increase ferry range. Theoretically it has been cleared for a variety of offensive stores up to and including Hellfire, but these are not considered necessary for general issue at this time.

61

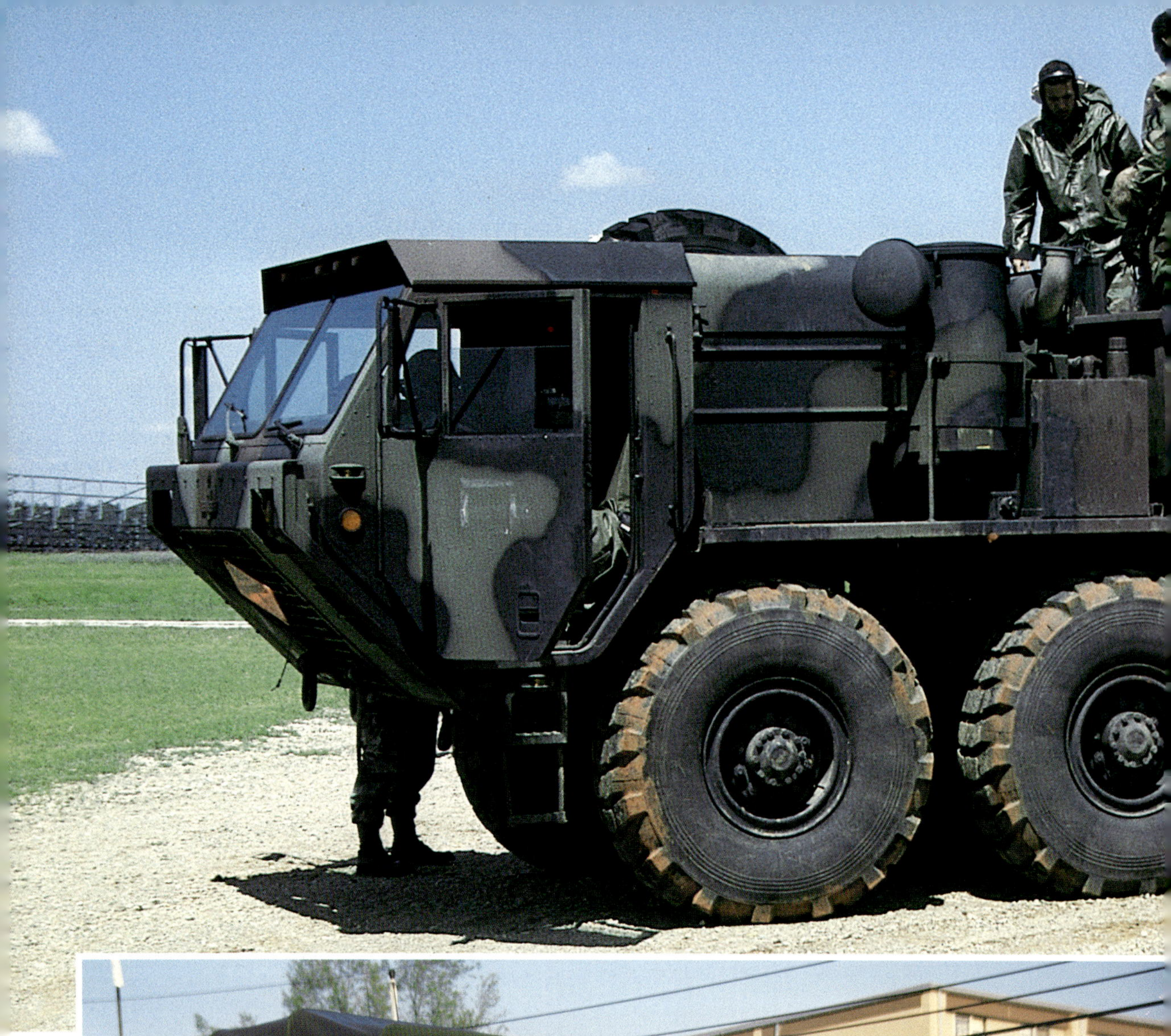

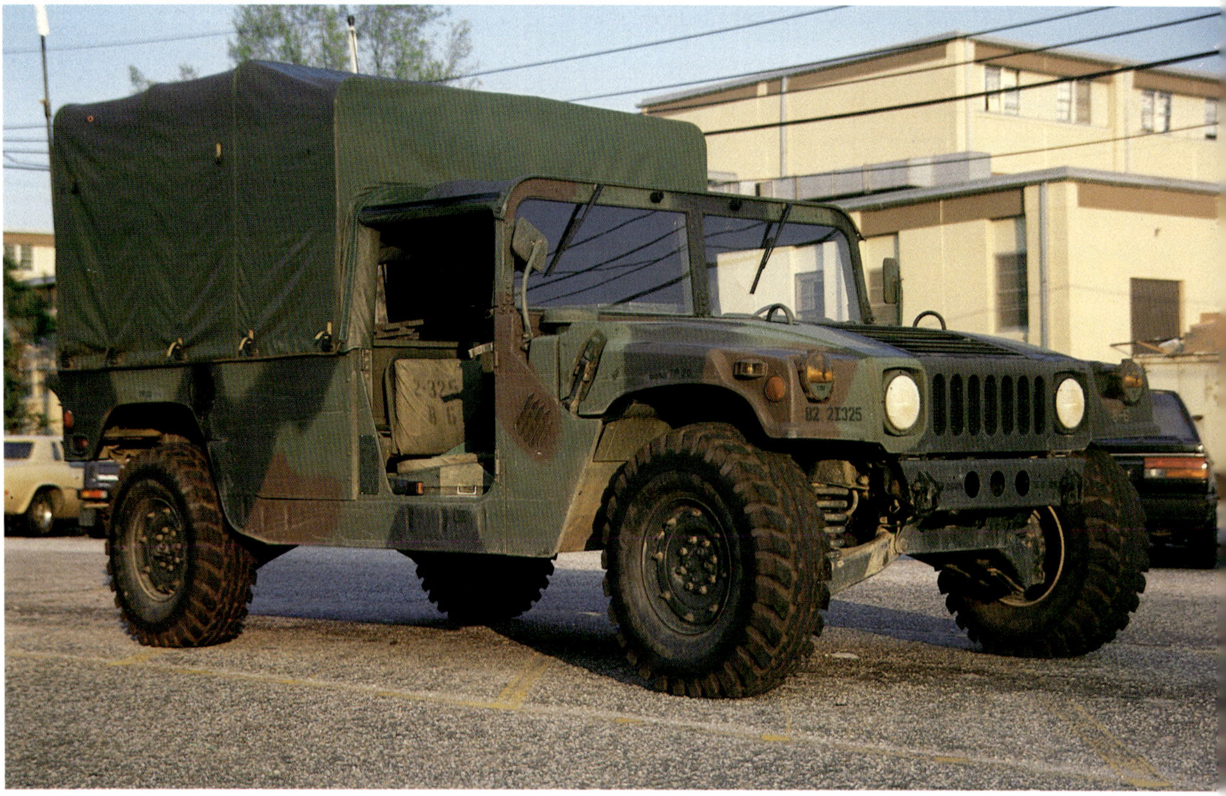

Supplementing and partially replacing vintage M35 'deuce-and-a-half' and newer 5-ton M939 trucks is the 10-ton 8x8 'Hemmet' built by the Oshkosh company, who have wide experience with cross-country fire-fighting vehicles. The Division presently employs four variants; this is the M977 (or M985 – the difference lies in the capacity of the cargo crane at the rear) used to carry ammunition and ordnance directly to the front line: note the 'explosives' diamond. The same chassis serves for the M978 fuel servicing truck; the M984 recovery vehicle currently replacing the Division's 5-ton wreckers; and the M983 tractor unit, which can haul a wide range of different trailer bodies.

(Far left) The omni-present HMMWV 'Humm Vee' comes in a bewildering choice of flavors; at least seven versions serve with the 82nd, all of them deliverable by parachute, by air-landing, or slung beneath helicopters; this is the S-250 (M1037) shelter carrier. A newly-developed version mounting a battery of Stinger anti-aircraft missiles is on its way. With the crew seated low either side of the engine and transmission, the $1\frac{1}{4}$-ton diesel has a low CG.

(Left) The M557 command post variant of the M113, of which just three remain in service with the Division.

A vitally important aspect of modern warfare, convincingly demonstrated during 'Desert Storm,' is the electronic battle. Listening to your enemy's communications and transmissions (ComInt and SigInt) tells you what he's doing and where; jamming them disrupts his command and control, and masks your own intentions.

One physical manifestation in the 82nd Aviation Bde. is the EH-60 'Quick Fix' platform. Details are, of course, classified, but as it is known to be a line-of-sight system the Blackhawk's ability to carry it to high altitude obviously enhances it. The external excrescences include radar warning receivers and AN/ALQ-144 infra-red jammer; passive defense would include chaff/flare dispensers, as well as the US Army's standard black/green IR-absorbent paint scheme, engine intake guards and exhaust plume suppressors.

The EH-60 is normally a creature of the night; here it was silhouetted at dawn as the sun broke over the dogwoods. Over in the camera ship, with the doors off and the chill morning air in our faces, we simply enjoyed one of those moments when you know for sure that life is worth living.

(Left) There is always a price to pay for freedom, and the 82nd Airborne have paid their share. 'Panama' was recently added to the memorial that stands outside the museum: there will doubtless be other additions by the time this book appears.

Acknowledgements

To all the men and women of the 82nd, who universally made me welcome and went to great trouble to ensure I got the pictures I needed during my two visits to Fort Bragg, my eternal gratitude. Thanks are due in particular to a number of individuals including Maj. Gen. Carl W. Stiner and latterly Maj. Gen. Richard Timmins, the Divisional Commanding Generals; Lt. Col. David R. Kiernan of XVIII Airborne Corps; Maj. N. Baxter Ennis, Capts. Deirdre Cozzens and Mike Phillips, Lt. Mary Jane Wardel, and many others at the 82nd's PAO; CW3 Karl Ebert, and all the aircrews who participated in the air-to-air sessions; Randy Jolly, Gordon Rottman, Dennis Baldry, Bob Morrison, and others who know who they are, for advice, assistance and support; Francois Vauvillier and Yves Debay, for help with recent Gulf photographs; and finally my wife and children, for remarkable patience and understanding.

For the technically-minded, the photos were taken with Canon T-90 and F-1 cameras using a variety of lenses from 28 to 400mm; film was primarily Kodak K-64, apart from those murky moments when 200 or 400 ASA had to be used. Unless otherwise credited in individual captions, all photos are by the author.

© 1991 Mike Verier

Printed in Singapore

This edition published in Great Britain 1991 by
Windrow & Greene Ltd.
5 Gerrard Street,
London W1V 7LJ

All rights reserved. No part of this publication may be reproduced or transmitted in any form or by any means electronic or mechanical, including photocopy, recording, or in any information storage and retrieval system, without the prior written permission of the publishers.

British Library Cataloguing in Publication Data
Verier, Mike
   82nd airborne division in colour photographs.–
(Europa-militaria)
I. Title II. Series
358.400973

ISBN 1-872004-85-7